PRAYERS TO PRAY COME RAIN OR SHINE

STEPHEN C. VANLANDINGHAM

Prayers To Pray Come Rain or Shine
By Stephen C. Vanlandingham
ISBN: 978-1-7333611-1-8
Copyright © 2020 by Stephen C. Vanlandingham
All publishing rights belong exclusively to Stephen C. Vanlandingham
Editor/Publisher: Stephen C. Vanlandingham
Published by: Printserve
Pensacola, Florida · 32526
scvan50@gmail.com
Cover Design: Pat Vanlandingham

TABLE OF CONTENTS

PRAYER 1 - ALWAYS PRAY

Holy Father, help me to always pray with excitement, fearless faith and great expectations. Help me to pray hopefully, joyfully, faithfully and lovingly without any doubts or reservation.

Teach me today how to enter your gates with thanksgiving, how to come into your courts with praise, how to worship you in spirit and in truth. How to pray without ceasing. In Jesus' name. Amen.

PRAYER 2 - PRAYER OF AGREEMENT

Precious Jesus, you taught us The Lord's Prayer. You taught us to pray, "Thy will be done." Now teach us how to pray The Prayer of Agreement:

"That if two of you shall agree on earth as touching any thing that they shall ask, it shall be done for them of my Father which is in heaven. For where two or three gather in my name, I am there with them." Amen.

PRAYER 3 - PRAYER OF FAITH

Holy Spirit, teach me how to pray the Prayer of Faith so that when I lay my hands upon the sick, the Lord will raise them up. And if they have committed sins, they will be forgiven. Amen.

PRAYER 4 - VOCABULARY OF PRAYER

Holy Spirit, teach me the vocabulary of praise. Teach me the worship words for my Lord Jesus: "I adore you. I bless your name. I delight in the glory of your presence. I exalt you above all others. I give you all the praise, all the honor and all the splendor due your name." Amen.

PRAYER 5 - PRAYER OF PREPOSITIONS

Holy Father, while stress, fear, danger and pestilence are all around us, help us to realize and remember that your Holy Spirit is within us. Your hand of power rests upon us, that you yourself go before us, your everlasting arms are underneath us, your tender mercies and forgiveness are behind us.

Almighty God, your everywhere presence is all around us, your majesty on high is above us, your heavenly angels are below us to catch us when we fall apart, you never leave us nor forsake us because you always walk beside us.

So, Lord God, if you be for us, who or what shall be against us, for nothing in heaven or on earth shall separate us from the Love of God which is in our Lord Jesus Christ! Amen!

PRAYER 6 - OUTSTRETCHED ARMS

Holy Father, I exalt you, I adore you, I bless your holy name. You are all wise, all knowing and everywhere present. Where can I go that your compassion and outstretched arms are not already there?

Thank you Lord, that you miraculously chose to make your infinite power perfect in our weakness.

PRAYER 7 - DOUBTS AND FEARS

Dear God, please help me. My doubts and fears have entangled me. I'm caught in-between being overwrought by my yesterdays and overanxious about my tomorrows. I'm mixed up and confused.

Please help me to know what to let go of and what to hang on to. Give me wisdom to know what matters most and what matters not at all. In Jesus' name.

PRAYER 8 - LET GO OF FAILURES

Holy Father, help me to keep my faith strong and let go of my failures. Help me to recount my victories, let go of my defeats and cling to your every promise.

Help me to forget about my setbacks and focus on the step backs I need to take that will empower me to stay anchored and grounded in you. Amen.

PRAYER 9 - UNCERTAINTIES

Holy Father, in spite of the uncertainties, insecurities and indecisions that are lying in wait before me, I press on toward the mark for the prize of the high calling of God in Christ Jesus. Amen.

PRAYER 10 - FAITH IS A FORCE

Holy Father, I keep forgetting. I need reminding. Remind me that faith is not a feeling, it's a force. It's not what I can see in front of me, it's what I can see inside of me. Not what I see in my mind's mind, but what I see in my heart's mind. Amen.

PRAYER 11 - THEE, THOU AND THINE

Holy Father, deliver me from my self-seeking, self-serving attitude. Help me to reset my focus away from I, me and mine and make it instead about Thou, Thee, and Thine. In Jesus' name I pray. Amen.

PRAYER 12 - SILENT BONDAGE

Holy Father, you are my Lord and God. I exalt you and praise your name forever and evermore. In perfect faithfulness you have done wonderful things for me. You bind up the broken-hearted. You open up the battened doors. Behind are those in silent bondage to depression and despair. You set the captives free. In Jesus' name. Amen.

PRAYER 13 - BRUISED AND WOUNDED HEART

Lord Jesus, with blazing voice you scream out to demons, "Go! You foul spirits!" Then, deep from the well of your bruised, wounded heart, you look to the seeker with their outstretched hand and say, "Who touched me?" "Lord, it's me." In Jesus' name. Amen.

PRAYER 14 - MY ARM OF STRENGTH

Oh Lord, only you can deliver me from the weight of my sins that hinder me and drag me down. You are my right hand. You are my arm of strength. You are the solid rock on which I stand. I praise and worship your holiness forever. Amen.

PRAYER 15 - COMING IN THE CLOUDS

Lord Jesus Christ, one day you are coming in the clouds of glory. Every eye will behold you. All the people of the earth will weep in your presence. Make me ready always to stand before you.

Only your blood on the Cross can hide my wrongdoings and spare me God's righteous judgments. In your holy name I pray. Amen.

PRAYER 16 - ROCKS BREAK THEIR SILENCE

Almighty God, Creator of the universe, let the rocks break their silence and shout for joy. All the birds of the air, all the fish of the sea, every living thing on the ground and in the trees sing their loud and silent praises to you, Oh our God.

All of the heavenly array, sun, moon and stars, bow at your feet. Exalt him everything in orbit around the universe. The circles inside every atom dance around your forever and everlasting throne. Praise to The Lord Most High. Amen.

PRAYER 17 - WINDS CLAP THEIR HANDS

Thunder from the west, crash your cymbals of loud exclaim. Lightening from the east, reveal the glory of the Son of his righteousness. Winds and rains clap their hands in joyful praise. Amen and Amen.

PRAYER 18 - CONFIDENT EXPECTATIONS

Holy Father, help me to come to you with confident expectation. I know you will answer every prayer I pray according to your will. Help me to be patient and realize that your perfect timing may be sooner or later. In Jesus' name. Amen.

PRAYER 19 - PLANT THE SEEDS OF HOPE

Holy Father, help me to touch at least one person today with your caring, compassion and kindness. Let the words I speak, the thoughts I think and the things I do plant in them the seeds of hope, joy and peace that will change their lives forever. In Jesus' name I pray. Amen.

PRAYER 20 - ETERNAL RICHES

Lord Jesus, you are my faithful provider of all I need. Not just of the material things of this life, but the eternal riches of joyfulness in spite of sadness, love in spite of hatred, hope instead of despair, of peace in the midst of turmoil and tenderness instead of indifference. In Jesus' name. Amen.

PRAYER 21 - THROUGH YOUR EYES

Lord, help me to discover the richness of your glory, your compassion and mercy. Let your forgiveness, faithfulness, hope and mercy be my constant assurance.

Help me to look at others through your eyes and see what

you see, instead of what I see in me. Amen.

PRAYER 22 - PRAISE YOU ENOUGH

Forgive me God because I can't worship you enough, I can't praise you enough, or thank you enough for your faithfulness and lovingkindness that you have gifted to me and all of your children. In Jesus' name. Amen.

PRAYER 23 - FORGIVE MY SINS

Lord Jesus Christ, Son of God, have mercy upon me. Forgive me of my sins of neglecting your words and commandments to love the Lord my God with all of my heart, with all of my soul, with all of my strength and with all of my might. Lord God, have mercy upon me. Amen.

PRAYER 24 - GUIDE MY EVERY FOOTSTEPS

Holy Spirit, fill me to overflowing with all of your fullness. Strengthen me with the power of your gracious anointing and indwelling. Guide my every footsteps along the light of your pathways. Amen.

PRAYER 25 - EVEN MY ENEMIES

Holy Father, help me to love those around me, my family and friends, my neighbors, even the stranger and my enemies, help me to love them as I love myself. In the name of Jesus I pray. Amen.

PRAYER 26 - PURE BY THE BLOOD

Father, I truly hunger and thirst after the kingdom of your righteousness. Make me pure by the blood of your Son, Jesus Christ my Lord and Savior. Amen.

PRAYER 27 - YOU CRUSHED YOUR SON

O my God, I can hardly fathom how it was your pleasure to crush your son and cause him to suffer. But he was wounded for my transgressions, bruised for my iniquities, punished so that I might have peace and by whose stripes I am healed. In your mighty name. Amen.

PRAYER 28 - THE POWER AND THE GLORY

Holy Father, all praise, honor and glory are yours forever, for Thine is the kingdom and the power and the glory forever. Amen and Amen.

PRAYER 29 - QUIET MY RACING THOUGHTS

Holy Father, please quiet my racing thoughts. In this very moment help me to slow down and be calm. Help me to accept today just as it is and not try to fix it or sort it all out. I will trust in you with all of my heart, all my soul, all of my strength and all of my mind. Amen.

PRAYER - 30 CONTROL MY ANGER

Holy Father, help me to take control of my anger when it begins to well up inside of me. Quiet my tongue, guard my lips from speaking profanities and words that bring pain and hurt to those who hear me.

Holy Spirit, distract my focus away from my rage and agitations that try to overwhelm me and overcome me. Rather, turn my words of frustration and indignation into words of love and compassion. In Jesus' name. Amen.

PRAYER 31 - THOSE WHO MISTREAT ME

Holy Father, I want to be a gentle and selfless person. I want to be kindhearted and forgiving of those who mistreat me with constant put-downs and lies.

Protect me from having an attitude of begrudging and resentment. Help me to always be a peacemaker, forgiving, accepting and understanding. Amen.

PRAYER 32 - Keep A Right Spirit

God and Father of our Lord Jesus Christ, I want to please you in everything I think, say and do. Give me the power of your Holy Spirit to help me keep a right spirit and attitude. In Jesus' name. Amen.

PRAYER 33 - OUTBURSTS OF BITTERNESS

Lord Jesus Christ, Son of God, have mercy upon me. Give me a humble and contrite heart that will cause me to forgive those who have brought out my outburst of bitterness and resentment. Instead of contempt, help me to speak your favor and blessings. In Jesus' name. Amen.

PRAYER 34 - My Failures

Father, because of my failures, help me not to wallow in my guilt and self-condemnation. Help me to repent quickly so that your warmth of compassion and mercy will overflow inside of me.

Fill me with all joy and peacefulness so it will well up my mind and emotions and entire being. In your precious name. Amen.

PRAYER 35 - THIS IS HOLY GROUND

Lord Jesus, hush my spirit within, quietly ease my racing heartbeats. Help me to realize that this is holy ground I'm standing on, and these circumstances are the sanctuary where you want me to worship you in Spirit and in truth. Amen.

PRAYER 36 - JOYFUL HAPPENINGS

Lord God, I pray that you will bestow me with expectations of favorable outcomes and joyful happenings. You said you are the Father of every good and perfect gift and you long to be gracious to your children. I receive your words. In Jesus' name. Amen.

PRAYER 37 - MOVE FOWARD IN FAITH

Holy Father, help me to move forward in my faith today instead of lagging behind in my doubts and distrust. Amen.

PRAYER 38 - We Are Your Receivers

Jesus, you are the giver of eternal life, we are your receivers. Hallelujah! You are the Lord our God. You reign forever. Amen.

PRAYER 39 - WANDERING MIND

Holy Spirit, you are my comforter and guide. When my mind begins to wander astray, help me to reign it back in with thoughts of joy and thanksgiving for all the things you have done for me. In your precious name. Amen.

PRAYER 40 - UNDERSERVING AS I AM

Holy Father, as undeserving as I am, you said that your goodness and mercy will follow me all the days of my life and I will live in your house forever. Thank you in Jesus' name. Amen.

PRAYER 41 - HURTING AND ALONENESS

Holy Father, help me to see things through your spirit eyes. Help me to show kindness and compassion to those I meet who are struggling within.

Help me to sense their hurting and aloneness and reach out my hand and not just my heart. Help me to set them free. Amen.

PRAYER 42 - THE SAD TO SMILE

Lord Jesus, give me your greatest joy today so that I will cause the sad to smile and the downcast to look up. In Jesus' name I pray. Amen.

PRAYER 43 - UNCONDITIONAL ACCEPTANCE

Father, some people feel worthless. Let me be the one to assure them that you love them, and value them, and accept them unconditionally. I want to be your light upon the hill, so they will glorify you, our Father in heaven. Amen.

PRAYER 44 - THE MAN'S HAND CLOUD

Holy Father, give me eyes of faith to see beyond what seems to be impossibilities and the unlikely. Instead of spiritual drought and despair, help me to behold a cloud the size of a man's hand and the armies of heaven marching beside me toward victory and triumph. In Jesus' name. Amen.

PRAYER 45 - ADORNED IN PURITY

Lord Jesus Christ, Son of God, come quickly. Come in golden splendor, in awesome majesty, exalted in power and glory, adored in purity. Amen.

PRAYER 46 - IN SPITE OF ME

I worship you Almighty God, Savior, Redeemer. I adore and praise your name. I love you Lord and I lift my voice. Thank you for loving me, understanding me and accepting me in spite of me. In Jesus' name. Amen.

PRAYER 47 - HEAVEN BOWS

Lord God, the King of Glory. Splendor, praise and adoration are yours alone. There is none like you. You are awesome and exalted in every way. All the mighty host of heaven bows and adores you. Amen and Amen.

PRAYER 48 - COMMAND MY MIND

God and Father of our Lord Jesus Christ, let your Holy Spirit command my mind and thoughts and desires. Saturate my entire being with all you wish and hope for me to be. I pray in the mighty name of Jesus, our Lord and King. Amen.

PRAYER 49 - YOUR EVER-LOVING KINDNESS

Lord Jesus Christ, thank you for shedding your blood and paying the price for all and every sin for all time. Your sacrifice is the glory and majesty of your love for our heavenly Father. Amen and Amen.

PRAYER 50 - FROM MY SINS

Thank you Lord. You separated me from my sins as far as the east is from the west. You trampled them beneath your footsteps and cast them into the depths of the sea to remember again no more. I praise you forever and ever. Amen.

PRAYER 51 - THE SUNRISE EACH MORNING

Thank you Father for the sunrise you give me each morning. Your joyfulness all through the day. Your promises are for a lifetime. Hallelujah! I praise you and say, Great and mighty is the Lord our God. Amen.

PRAYER 52 - GIVING ME PURPOSE

Thank you Holy Spirit for giving me purpose. You have called me to do your good will and proclaim your good news of forgiveness and healing and deliverance. Amen.

PRAYER 53 - NOT DONE WITH ME YET

Thank you Lord that you are not done with me yet, you've empowered me to show forth the praises of Him who has called me out of darkness into his marvellous light. Amen.

PRAYER 54 - A LIFE WEIGHED DOWN

Holy Father, help me to always keep watch and be ready. You said you will come when no one is expecting. God, forbid that I would live a life weighed down with worldly anxieties and be caught unprepared of your sudden presence. In Jesus' name. Amen.

PRAYER 55 - GLORIOUS APPEARING

Holy Father, I wait for the day of your Son's glorious appearing, when every knee shall bow and every tongue confess that Jesus Christ is Lord to the glory of God our Father. Amen

PRAYER 56 - I RAISE MY HANDS.

Holy Father, I lift up my head, I raise up my hands, blind me to everything else I see. Open my heart and seal my lips to hear you say, "Do not be afraid, I am with you. Do not lose heart, I will strengthen you." O Lord, I give you all my praise. Amen.

PRAYER 57 - MY RIGHTEOUS RIGHT HAND

Holy Spirit, I hear your voice calling me, "I am your teacher and I will teach you. I am your guide and I will guide you into all truth. I am your comforter and I will not leave you comfortless.

I am your constant companion. I will ever walk beside you. I will ever dwell within you. I will empower you. I will defend you against all your enemies. I will uphold you with the power of my righteous right hand." In Jesus' holy name. Amen.

Prayer 58 - What Can I Say

Holy Father, what can I say? If God be for us, who can be against us? For thine is the kingdom and the power and the glory, forever, Amen.

Prayer 59 - My Disease

Holy Father, I am sick and I may not get well. My disease is overtaking me little by little each day. Yet, in spite of it all, my hope is firm in you.

Lord, help my faith to become stronger, more than ever in my troubled life. Help me to trust you and know that you are with me, right beside me in every move I try to take. Amen.

Prayer 60 - Doubts And Despair

Holy Father, I know you haven't forgotten nor forsaken me, and you never will. Thank you, Holy Spirit, for living within me, comforting me and praying for me. As I struggle with doubts and despair, enlighten me to see you in every dark corner of my life. In Jesus' name. Amen.

Prayer 61 - Settle My Emotions

Lord Jesus Christ, Son of God, have mercy upon me. Let your perfect peace settle upon my mind and emotions, my body, soul and spirit, my entire being. In Jesus' name. Amen.

Prayer 62 - Battle For My Life

Help me O God, to praise you, worship you, adore you and exalt you so that your name is highly lifted up in spite of this battle for my life that is raging inside of me.

Holy Father, make me strong and courageous, unwavering in my trust and hope in you. Give me your peace that transcends all understanding to guard my heart and my mind. Amen.

PRAYER 63 - I CONFESS MY SINS

Lord Jesus, I confess to you my sins of anger and disappointment. I know that you are the Father of compassion and the God of all comfort, and you understand me perfectly. Amen.

PRAYER 64 - YESTERDAY MOMENTS

Holy Father, help me to leave the yesterday moments and the tomorrow moments where they are, while I focus on the today moments where I already am. For This is the day that the Lord has made, and I will rejoice and be glad in it. Amen!

PRAYER 65 - THROUGH ALL MY FEARS

God and Father of our Lord Jesus Christ, I praise you with my whole heart. With everything within me I worship you and I adore you forever and ever.

Holy Father, give me a sense of your perfect love, your presence, and your mighty strength to empower me through all of my doubts and fears. In Jesus' name. Amen.

PRAYER 66 - MY RAGING STORM

Lord Jesus, during the raging storm you spoke the words, "Peace be still." And the seas became glass. Savior, Redeemer, speak those words to my heart today. All praise is yours forever. Amen and Amen.

PRAYER 67 - BURDENS AND ANXIETIES

Father in heaven, I love you, I trust you, I put all of my hope in you. Help me to cast all of my burdens and anxieties upon you and not try to figure things out or trust in my own strength. Be strong in the Lord, and in the power of his might. Amen!

Prayer 68 - To Stand Firm

Lord Jesus, as I begin to sway toward doubts, help me to seek you and your righteous Kingdom first, your forgiveness and compassion, your peace that passes all understanding, your courage to stand firm and your words of power and comfort. In Jesus' name. Amen.

Prayer 69 - My Sickness

Holy Father, in my sickness today, let me hear you say to me, "Your faith has healed you, go in peace and be freed from your sins." Amen.

Prayer 70 - Authority Through Christ

Holy Father, You are our only God and Savior. Your's is the majesty, the power and the authority, through Jesus Christ our Lord. Amen.

Prayer 71 - You Bring Out The Wind

Merciful Father, King of Glory, Lord God Almighty. When you speak, you cause the clouds to ascend from the ends of the earth. You make lightning from the rain, you bring out the wind from your storehouses, you speak with the voice of thunder.

Behold our God, Maker and Creator of everything that is, has been and forever and ever will be. Amen.

Prayer 72 - Mercy And Forgiveness

King of kings, Lord of lords, you long to be gracious. You rise up to show compassion for you are the God of all comfort. Love, mercy and forgiveness you freely give. Amen.

Prayer 73 - You Rescue Us

Holy Father, your name is exalted. We can only hope in you.

You are our deliverer, only you can rescue us and set us free from death, hell and the grave. And so shall we ever be with the Lord. Amen.

PRAYER 74 - OVERFLOW US WITH FAITH

Holy Father, without you there is despair and hopelessness. But God of hope, fill us with all joy and peace as we trust in you so that we may overflow with faith, hope and love by the power of Your Holy Spirit. Amen.

PRAYER 75 - KEEP ON ASKING

Father in heaven, we ask and keep on asking. We knock and keep on knocking. We seek and keep on seeking. We will not give up our pursuit for your righteous kingdom. Amen.

PRAYER 76 - ALWAYS KEEP ME READY

Lord Jesus Christ, only begotten Son of the Father, we look for your coming in the clouds of glory. Always keep me ready to stand by the blood of your holiness before our God, the righteous judge. Give me clean hands and a pure heart as I surrender myself to you with all of my worship. Amen.

PRAYER 77 - LET GO OF MY WEAKNESS

Holy Father, help me to realize that though I am powerless, you are powerful. Help me to grasp your strength and let go of my weakness. Fill my mind with thoughts of you and empty my heart of the doubts and negativity I think about myself. Amen.

PRAYER 78 - WHAT IF WITH I AM

Lamb of God, help me to answer every "What if?" With your "I am."

I am the bread of life. I am the way, the truth and the life. I am the light of the world. I am the door. I am the good shepherd. I am the resurrection and the life.

Lo, I am with you always, even to the end of the age. Amen and Amen.

PRAYER 79 - WILL AND PURPOSE FOR ME

Holy Spirit, help me to open my eyes so I can see you, my ears so I can hear you, my heart so I can feel you, my entire being so I can experience the fullness of your perfect will and purpose for my life. In Jesus' name. Amen.

PRAYER 80 - CLOUDING MY VISION

My God, Father of our Lord Jesus Christ, take away the scales from my eyes that are clouding my vision from seeing what you want me to see.

Show me your love and compassion, your mercy and forgiveness, your quiet presence and the fullness of what it means to walk in the Spirit, and worship you in Spirit and in truth. Amen.

PRAYER 81 - OUR MILITARY

Holy Father, I pray for all of our military troops who sacrifice their lives to save ours. Every day they take their stand in stations and deployments all over the world so that we can live safe and secure and enjoy our freedoms and liberties. Thank you for them. Amen.

PRAYER 82 - OUR MILITARY, PROTECT THEM

Father, set a constant watch and guard over those who set a constant guard and watch over us every sleeping and waking hour of the day. Protect our troops who protect us, keep them safe, make them bold in battle, courageous and fearless against all of our enemies. In Jesus' name. Amen.

PRAYER 83 - OUR MILITARY, COURAGEOUS

Holy Father, thank you for our airmen, soldiers and seaman, from the lowest to the highest rank. Pour out upon them your great mercy and compassion, your forgiveness and salvation. Bring them to prayer in every need.

May they always call out to you in their moments of despair and darkness. In their unbearable times. Flood their hearts with your almighty peace, courage and confidence. In Jesus' name. Amen.

PRAYER 84 - OUR MILITARY FAMILIES

God, bless our troops wherever they may be. Let us not just salute them, but honor them and take our greatest pride in their humble strength to serve every citizen, good or bad, adoring or defiant, gracious or forgotten.

Father, help us as their nation, to humble ourselves before their families at home, their wives and husbands, their children and parents and all the others who have to live without them for months, sometimes years at the time.

Lord, some of them come home to babies they've never seen or held and they're already walking and talking. My God, never let these courageous loved ones feel alone or forgotten around us. In Jesus' name. Amen.

PRAYER 85 - MILITARY - FALLEN SOLDERS

Lord God Almighty, when the taps sound over our fallen soldiers' lives, may our floodgate of tears and emotions elevate them to the highest ranks in glory.

Savior, Lord Jesus, as you died to make us holy. Let these live to keep us free. And our troops keep marching on. Amen!

PRAYER 86 - RECEIVE RESURRECTION

Lord Jesus Christ, Son of God, have mercy upon me. Forgive me of all the wrongs I commit, the faithless words I speak and the selfish things I do.

I kneel at your cross and repent. I raise my hands at your empty tomb and receive resurrection of the body and life everlasting. Amen.

PRAYER 87 - COUNTLESS MIRACLES

Holy Father, your name is exalted and worthy to be praised. You perform miracles we cannot count, wonders we cannot comprehend. You bring death back to life and everything you make, you create out of nothing. Amen and Amen.

PRAYER 88 - IN MY EMOTIONS

Holy Spirit, in the middle of all my darkness, help me to put my complete hope in you. Help me to believe in you in all of my thinking. Help me to trust in you with all of my emotions. Help me to yield to you in all of my doings. In your precious name. Amen.

PRAYER 89 - ENFEEBLED BODY

Holy Father, blind my eyes so that all I see is your greatness and goodness. Deafen my ears so that all I hear are your words of comfort and forgiveness. Lord God, enfeeble my body so that I can only be strong in your strength and the power of your might. Amen.

PRAYER 90 - THROUGH DOORS OF DOUBT

Holy Spirit of God, help me to break through the doors of doubt by the prayers I pray and your words that I hide in my heart that I might not sin against you.

Help me to filter out all the bad in my life by clinging to the precious blood Jesus shed on the cross. Amen.

PRAYER 91 - NO ROOM LEFT

My Lord and Savior, overflow me with all of the fullness of your compassion and loving care, so that there is no room left in me for dispassion and indifference. Amen.

PRAYER 92 - SWEET DELIVERANCE

Tender shepherd, forever cradle me in the arms of your sweet deliverance. Let it be. Let it be. Amen.

PRAYER 93 - PRAYER FOR MY CHILDREN

Holy Father, I pray for my children today that they will develop a passion for the things of God. Help them to always hunger and thirst for your righteous kingdom in their life.

I pray that they will look to your Holy Word to lead them in all of their life decisions. I pray that they will love you with all of their heart, mind, soul and being. Give them a compassionate and generous heart to love others in the way that you love them. In Jesus' name. Amen.

PRAYER 94 - PRAYER FOR MY CHILDREN

Holy Father, help my children to make choices that will bring your favor and blessings into their life. Protect them from everything evil that comes against them. Give them the gift of discerning of spirits to recognize what is wrong, ungodly things and people, and resist them through the power of your Holy Spirit.

I pray that they will always seek your forgiveness, be humble and sensitive to their own wrongdoings and know that you love them and accept them no matter what. Amen.

Prayer 95 - A Prayer For My Children

Holy Father, help my children to be a shining example and model of respect, dignity and integrity in every word they speak, every thought they think, and everything they do.

Let their lights so shine before men that they may see their good works and glorify their Father in heaven. Amen.

Prayer 96 - Prayer For My Children

Son of God, I pray for my children. Help them to develop a grateful heart so that they will always be quick to thank you for every good thing in their life.

When bad things come, help them to still give you thanks and know that you will deliver them from all evil and bring them through whatever hardship or trials they may face. Amen.

Prayer 97 - Prayer For My Children

Holy Spirit, empower my children with your wisdom and understanding. Help them to not be intimidated by anyone who would try to bully them and push them to compromise their values and convictions.

Instead, make them bold, courageous, and rock solid in their faith in you, immovable, unshakeable and unwavering. Let them always experience your peace, joy and love and never lose their way as they walk in the paths of righteousness for your namesake. In your precious name. Amen.

Prayer 98 Every Knee Shall Bow

Holy Father, I exalt and adore your name. Your name is above all names. At the mention of your name every knee bows and every tongue confesses that you are the Lord God Almighty. Amen!

PRAYER 99 - GIFT OF DISCERNMENT

Lord Jesus, fill me today with all of your acts of kindness, your mercy, compassion and grace. Gift me with the Spirit of discernment so that I will know those around me who need my care and kindness. In Jesus' name. Amen.

PRAYER 100 - LORD JESUS, COVER ME

Holy Father, cover me with your protecting hands and keep me safe from all harm and evil attacks against me. Cover me with your presence. Cover me with your righteousness. Cover me with your holiness. Lord Jesus, cover me. Amen.

PRAYER 101 - ONLY SPEAK YOUR WORDS

Father, Help me to speak only the words that you want me to speak, help me to do only the things you want me to do, help me to be all that you are and want me to be. Amen.

PRAYER 102 - COMMAND MY MIND

Lord God Almighty, command my mind and thoughts and desires. Let the light of your presence shine upon me so that your hope, love and joy surrounds me from every side, above me and below me, before me and behind me. On my right hand and on my left. Amen.

PRAYER 103 - MY MAIN EVENT TODAY

Lord Jesus Christ, Son of God, have mercy upon me. Be my main event today and not my second thought. Be my first priority and not my last resort. Be my guide and sure direction, so that all of my footsteps fall gently inside all of your footprints. Let my life be a shing light to everyone around me. Amen.

PRAYER 104 - YOUR EVERY GOOD GIFT

Lord God, I bow my head to reverence your holiness. I raise my hands to receive your righteousness. I close my eyes and ears to block out all of the sights and sounds of wicked worldliness.

Holy Father, I open my heart and mind to be filled with your grace and every good and perfect gift that comes down from the Father of lights. In Jesus' name. Amen.

PRAYER 105 - COME IN GILDEN SPLENDOR

God, Almighty God, come in golden splendor, and awesome majesty, exalted in power and glory, adorned in purity. Amen.

PRAYER 106 - DESTROY EVERY STRONGHOLD

Holy God and Father of our Lord Jesus Christ, I thank you for the cleansing blood of your Son over my heart and mind today. Rebuke and pull down every stronghold that tries to exalt itself against the wisdom and knowledge of your majesty and glory in my life. Amen.

PRAYER 107 - IN PAIN AND CONFUSION

Holy Father, purify me and renew a right spirit within me. Help me to listen to your Word. Teach me how to worship you in the midst of pain and confusion and not just in the good times of blessings and prosperity. In your precious name. Amen.

PRAYER 108 - COMPASSIONATE HANDS

Holy Spirit, guide me and empower me to be a compassionate witness of your love and tenderness to those around me who are fragile and weak and suffering in their brokenheartedness.

Help me to discern who they are and what they are feeling and how I can touch them, not just with my heart, but with caring and compassionate hands. Amen.

PRAYER 109 - PLEASE SET ME FREE

Holy Father, you said that you set the captives free. Please set me free. You said that you would never reject a broken and contrite heart. Lord, that's all I have to offer you today, the sacrifice of my broken and contrite heart. Lord, overflow my heart with your joy and peace, your calm and quietness. In Jesus' name. Amen.

PRAYER 110 - EVERY BEAT OF MY HEART

Holy Father, let every beat of my heart exalt you. Let every breath I breathe bring you joyful adoration. Let every blink of my eyes look upon Your majesty and proclaim, "Holy, holy, holy Lord, God of power and might, the whole earth is full of your glory!" Amen!

PRAYER 111 - SACKCLOTH OF SUFFERING

Lord Jesus Christ, Son of God, I will praise your name forevermore. You turn my cries of despair into shouts of victory. You remove the sackcloth of my suffering and clothe me with the garment of praise.

Holy Father, you adorn me with your robe of righteousness. You exalt me before the throne of your glory. I will sing eternal praises with all of the saints and holy ones forever and ever. We will bow down and cast our crowns of glory before your throne. Amen and Amen.

PRAYER 112 - SLEEP IN PERFECT SLEEP

Lord Jesus Christ, Son of God, only you Lord make me dwell in safety. I think of your great goodness and countless blessings. When I wake up in the night, I will bless your precious name.

I will remember the awesome and amazing things you have

done in my life. Everything I have ever needed, your hands have provided. Amen.

PRAYER 113 - WALK IN ABUNDANCE

Holy Father, surround me with your blessings and divine favor today. Pour out every good thing that is yours upon my life. Let me walk in the abundance of your grace and mercy and lovingkindness. Let the goodwill and favor of everyone I encounter today come upon me. In Jesus' name. Amen.

PRAYER 114 - COMPASSION AND ACCEPTANCE

Holy Father, help me to follow you in the way you want me to go. Help me to think your thoughts, speak your words and desire what you desire for me. Help me to be giving and kind and caring of others so that I will show them your compassion and acceptance and the love of Christ. In your precious name. Amen.

PRAYER 115 - MARVELOUS FAITH

Lord Jesus, fill me to overflowing with the great faith you marveled at in the centurion soldier. Let your springs of living water well up inside of me like the woman at the well. And in the words of your prophet, let me mount up with wings as eagles so I will run and not grow weary, I will walk and not faint. Amen.

PRAYER 116 - HURTING ALONE

Holy Father, help me to look at others through your eyes and have sincere compassion for those who are struggling and hurting and alone. Help me to reach out to them, not with vague words and a half heart, but with my whole heart full of caring, touching hands. Amen and Amen.

PRAYER 117 - BRING THEM SMILES

Holy Spirit, help me to take opportunities each day to encourage those who are struggling, and bring them smiles and assure them that they are valued and that others do care and want to help them.

Holy Father, help me to not dare claim to be walking in the spirit, until I've put feet on my prayers. In Jesus' name. Amen.

PRAYER 118 - HOPE BEYOND DOUBT

Holy Father, you are my strength and shield. You are my God Most High. You are the rock of my salvation. You are the possible in all of my impossibilities. Is there anything too hard for the Lord? Today I will reach out to you in faith beyond question, in hope beyond doubt and in love beyond measure. Amen.

PRAYER 119 - HEM OF YOUR GARMENT

Lord Jesus, as I touch the hem of your garment, heal me of all my sicknesses and deliver me from all my diseases. Say to me, "Your faith has made you whole, go in peace and be free from your afflictions." Then I will enter into your temple walking, and leaping, and praising God! Amen and Amen!

PRAYER 120 - GOD OF POWER AND MIGHT

Holy Father, your's is the greatness and the power and the glory and the splendor and the majesty forever and evermore. Holy, Holy, Holy Lord, God of power and might, heaven and earth are full of your glory. Let everything that has breath, praise the Lord! Amen!

PRAYER 121 - GOOD MORNING

Holy Father, you are my Alpha and Omega, my "Good Morning" and "Good Night." In all of todays, in-betweens, help me to be at my best, do my best and give my best to you and especially to those I will cross paths with along the way. In Jesus' name.

PRAYER 122 - CHANCE HAPPENINGS

Holy Spirit, help me to realize throughout the day that there are no by chance happenings to me. They are divine connections where I can be there for someone who needs me. I can believe in someone who has lost faith in themselves. I can befriend that someone who's feeling rejected and alone, and I can become that weak someone's strong arm and guiding light. Amen.

PRAYER 123 - OVERSHADOW YOU

And now may the Lord God Almighty direct his footsteps toward you, make his blessings indwell you, and his precious Holy Spirit overshadow and empower you. In Jesus' name. Amen.

PRAYER 124 - NAIL-SCARRED HANDS

Holy Father, let your gentleness absorb my unsettledness, your soothing touch my tenseness. Drown out all of my doubts and fears with a single drop of the tears you shed for me in your darkest hours on the Cross. I raise up my trembling hands to feel the touch of your reaching down, nail-scarred hands. Amen.

PRAYER 125 - LAW ENFORCEMENT

We pray and intercede for all of our courageous and honorable peacekeepers. May your divine righteousness guard our law enforcement community. Protect them. Shield and defend them.

We ask that in this moment you will dispatch legions of godly prayer warriors to kneel in repentance and humble contrition so that you will hear from heaven, forgive us our sins and heal our land. Lord Jesus Christ, Son of God, have mercy upon us. Amen.

PRAYER 126 - ALL DAY, EVERYDAY

Precious Jesus, I want all of the blessings you promised those who hunger and thirst after your righteousness. I want more than just a one-time spiritual event, I want the all-day, everyday, eight days a week days of your extraordinary majesty and magnificence. And now to the only God our Savior be glory, majesty, power and authority, through Jesus Christ our Lord. Amen.

PRAYER 127 - A CONTRITE HEART

Holy Father, as I kneel in prayer, I want to bring you the sacrifice of praise. But instead, all I have to offer is the sacrifice of a broken spirit and a contrite heart. You know the burden I'm carrying. You know the heaviness I feel. I want to give it all to you, but it's hard to let go. Please help me Lord. Amen.

PRAYER 128 - RAINBOW OF PROMISES

Holy Father, help me to stop seeing the wrongs behind me, and instead, see your rainbow of promises in front of me. Close my eyes to the army of my enemies, and instead, open them so I can see the hills full of horses and your chariots of fire! In Jesus' name. Amen.

PRAYER 129 - RUSHING MIGHTY WIND

Holy Father, instead of listening to confused voices, help me to listen to your still small voice. Instead of hearing empty sounds, help me to hear the sound of your mighty rushing wind filling the place where I stand. In your precious name. Amen.

PRAYER 130 - TREMBLING HANDS

Holy Father, help me to reach out my trembling hands so that I can touch the hem of your garment and be made whole. I don't want to just ride out the storm, I want to ride in your chariot of clouds on the winds of the storm! Amen!

PRAYER 131 - RIGHTEOUS RIGHT HAND

My faith is in you. I believe in you. I hope in you. You are my God in whom I trust. You uphold me with your righteous right hand. In Jesus' name I pray. Amen.

PRAYER 132 - PRAYER LIFE

Holy Father, I need your help with my prayer life. I want to learn how to pray only those prayers you will answer for me. You said that sometimes my prayers go silent because I waste them on wrong things. But then you said that as long as I keep seeking your righteous kingdom first, that you would keep on giving me everything I need, by your glorious riches in Christ Jesus. Amen.

PRAYER 133 - YOUR PERFECT PRAYER

Holy Father, thank you for teaching me your perfect prayer, The Lord's prayer. I pray it over and over again, no matter where I am, who I'm with, or what I'm doing. Sometimes I pray it loudly. Sometimes I sing it in a song. Mostly I just whisper it silently in my heart. Amen.

PRAYER 134 - IN MY DEEPEST WOES

Holy Father, I'm not here to ask you for something, I'm here to thank you for everything. You've done so much for me, there's nowhere to start. In every direction I see, you've always been there beside me. In my greatest joys and my deepest woes. In my happiest moments and my loneliest hours. Amen.

PRAYER 135 - YOU HELD MY HEART

Lord Jesus, rejection had been my cruelest enemy. Nothing else has belittled my spirit or beaten me down more than the indifference of this person I loved. Nothing has ever wounded my feelings more. I could never survive. But I have. When no one else was there to hold my hand, you were there and held my heart. Thank you. In Jesus' name. Amen.

PRAYER 136 - LONELINESS

Holy Father, help me in my loneliness. Speak to me when no one else is around to talk to. Take the hurtfulness out of my heart when I feel that no one else cares or ever thinks about me anymore.

Lord Jesus, fill the empty spaces in my heart left by those who are missing from my life. Death, distance, divorce, time have taken them away from me. Life has moved on for them, but left me behind.

Holy Spirit, only you can fill those voids and vacancies inside me. Help me to discover you in a new way, as constant companion, friend and guide. Miracles happen everyday. Make one happen for me, Lord. In Jesus' name.

PRAYER 137 - MY HEART TRUSTS IN YOU

Holy Father, you are my strength and shield. My heart trusts in you. My spirit is full of joy, I will worship you in prayers of thanksgiving. You are my God, I trust you and adore you forevermore. Amen.

PRAYER 138 - GOODWILL AND FAVOR

Holy Father, surround me with your blessings and divine favor today. Pour out every good thing that is yours upon my life.

Let me walk in the abundance of your grace and mercy and lov-ingkindness. And may the goodwill and favor of everyone I encounter today overflow upon my life. Amen!

PRAYER 139 - THE LEAP OF FAITH

Holy Father, I will never stop praising you for your mighty deeds and power to save. No one is like you! I want to run beyond the steps of faith and take the leap of faith into your deep mysteries you have called me to. Amen.

PRAYER 140 - BEYOND THE MOMENT

Holy Father, I don't want to just live in the moment, I don't want to just live for the moment, I want to live beyond the moment, overflowing with awesome excitement and expectancy. I want to live where you are doing a new thing, making a way in the wilderness and streams in the desert! Amen!

PRAYER 141 - MY SPIRITUAL FERVOR

Let me never be lacking in zeal, but keep my spiritual fervor, always serving you with my whole heart, mind and being. In Jesus' name I pray. Amen.

PRAYER 142 - ANXIOUS THOUGHTS

Thank you holy Father that all of my fearful and anxious thoughts melt away in the light of your wonderful presence. Fill me with thankfulness and let it overshadow all of my troublesome and guilt-ridden emotions from my past. Amen.

PRAYER 143 - MAKE MY NIGHTS GLOW

Almighty God, I praise you that your everlasting presence is your promise that I will never have to face anything alone. When darkness covers me, you make your light to shine around me. You make my nights glow like the brightness of the day. I worship you and adore you. Amen and Amen.

PRAYER 144 - WITHOUT EXCEPTION

Holy Father, fill me with your blessings. Overflow me with your favor and ever lovingkindness. Do a new thing in my life today. Lead me along new paths of discovery and revelation. Open my eyes so that I will see what you see when you look at me - valuable, the apple of your eye, acceptable without exception. In your precious name. Amen.

PRAYER 145 - YOU TRAMPLE MY SINS

Holy Father, help me to see how you love me with an everlasting love. In spite of my sins and failures and disobedience, you are patient, kind, full of mercy, always forgiving. You trample my sins under your feet and hurl my iniquities into the depths of the sea. Your compassion never fails. They are new every morning. Amen.

PRAYER 146 - THE BREATH OF THE DAWN

Lord God, you said you will raise me up on the breath of the dawn. You said you will hold me in the palm of your hand. You said you will make me to shine like the sun and your faithfulness will forever be my shield and protector.

Lord, you even said your angels will guard and protect me in all of my ways. When I fall down, they will lift me up. Holy Father, I believe you. I trust you. I hope in you. I love you. In Jesus's name. Amen.

PRAYER 147 - OVERSHADOW ME

Holy Father, unleash your mountain-moving faith in my life today! Help me to believe in my own worthiness to receive miracles from your wonder-working hands.

Overflow my heart and mind with unexplainable peace and a passion for holy living. Cover me with joyfulness. Overshadow me with your love. Holy Spirit, take hold of my trembling hand and guide me through every uncertainty and insecurity. Amen.

PRAYER 148 - THE ENTRY GATE

Lord God, I have made your scriptures the entry gate into every desire of my innermost being. Thy word is a lamp unto my feet, and a light unto my path. I have hidden thy word in my heart that I might not sin against you. In Jesus' name. Amen.

PRAYER 149 - I WILL FLOURISH

Holy Spirit, saturate my spiritual surroundings with the sound of your voice so that I will flourish in an environment of obedience and expectation. Give me the self-confidence and inner persuasion that I can accomplish every dream and goal you have laid out for my life. Amen.

PRAYER 150 - BRING ME BLESSINGS

Lord Jesus Christ, Son of God, overflow me with emotions of enthusiasm and excitement so that everything I do, everywhere I go and everything I think will bring me blessing, after blessing, after blessing of your holy goodness and divine favor. In Jesus' matchless name I pray. Amen.

PRAYER 151 - MAKING ALL THINGS NEW

How compassionate and merciful are you to exchange my ungodliness for your righteousness, my shame for your kindly sorrow, my condemnation for your justification.

You have promised us, behold I am making all things new. if any man be in Christ, he is a new creature. Old things are passed away, all things are become new. In Jesus' name. Amen.

PRAYER 152 - A PANDEMIC IS RISING

Holy Father, anxieties and stress are all around us. A murderous pandemic is rising up before us unchecked and unrestrained. Godless. Violent people are seeking to silence the very bedrock of law and order.

Lord God, even in the skies are troublesome sights. Storm clouds are gathering. The distress of nations is widening. Wickedness is about to give an account. But the righteous will stand forever! With bated breath we listen for the shout of the archangel and the trumpet call of God. Come Lord Jesus! Amen.

PRAYER 153 - PANIC ATTACK

Breathe on me breath of God. Holy Father, in this very moment, trample down this panic attack rearing itself up against me. Trample it to death! Destroy it. Command it to go now. Breathe on me breath of God. In Jesus' name. Amen.

PRAYER 154 - DREAD AND DESPAIR

Holy Father, crush over these fears and anxieties I'm feeling. Grind them into nothing. Breath on me breath of God.

Holy Spirit that raised up Christ from the dead, raise me up to soar high above these mountains of dread and despair. Breathe on me breath of God. Amen.

PRAYER 155 - GUIDE ME

Holy Father, I praise your mighty name. I thank you for all of your blessings and goodness upon my life. You guide me, you comfort me, you protect me, you empower me. So, I trust in you, I believe in you, I hope in you, and I love you with all of my heart, all of my soul, all of my strength and all of my mind. Amen.

PRAYER 156 - RELAX IN YOUR PRESENCE

Father, help me to relax in your presence today. Help me to let go of all of the anxious emotions and worries I have been wrestling with. Refresh my mind and thoughts and imagination, and cause quiet, calm and contentment to walk beside me every step of the way. In Jesus' name I pray. Amen.

PRAYER 157 - AURA OF ENTHUSIASM

Holy Father, give me the self-confidence and inner persuasion that I can accomplish the goals you have established for me. Create an aura of enthusiasm and expectation in every thought I think, in everything I do and everywhere I go. Amen.

PRAYER 158 - WE ARE READY

Lord God, storm clouds are gathering. The distress of nations is widening. Wickedness is about to give an account. But the righteous will stand forever! With bated breath we listen for the shout of an archangel and the trumpet call of God. We are ready.

We stand upon our feet. We raise up our hands. We lift up our voices, "Lord Jesus Christ, Son of God, come in Golden Splendor and awesome majesty, exalted in power and glory, adorned in purity." Amen.

PRAYER 159 - THE MIDDLE OF THE NIGHT

Holy Father, it's the middle of the night and I'm sitting here in the dark. I'm trying to leave my outcomes up to you, but I'm tired of wait and see. Don't you hear me crying out? Can't you at least give me a glimpse of some something that lies ahead? I need your spirit eyes. In Jesus' name. Amen.

PRAYER 160 - MY HANDS ARE TIED

Lord Jesus, I'm looking, but I can't see you with my eyes

closed. I'm listening, but I can't hear you with my ears silenced. I'm reaching out, but how can I touch you with my hands tied behind me? How can I feel your presence when my heart is broken? In Jesus name I pray. Amen.

PRAYER 161 - GRATITUDE IS THE GATE

Holy Father, You said that my gratitude is the gate into your presence and in my praise is where you live. So, I bow myself before you, that you will lift me up. I bless your name, so that you will bless my life. I give you my body, mind, soul and spirit, so that you will give me the power and presence of your Holy Spirit. In Jesus' name I pray. Amen.

PRAYER 162 - I AM A RECEIVER

Lord Jesus, one day you breathed on your disciples. You said, "Receive the Holy Spirit!" On another day you said, "And you will receive power when the Holy Spirit comes on you." Lord Jesus, I am your disciple. I am a receiver. Breathe on me your more than abundant, life-giving breath. Amen.

PRAYER 163 - A HUNDREDFOLD HARVEST

Holy Spirit of God, comfort me, counsel me, empower me, pray for me, protect me, provide for me, revive me, rejoice in me. Produce in me a hundredfold harvest of your boundless fruits: joyfulness, peacefulness, goodness, gentleness, faithfulness, self-lessness. And most of all, Lord, your forever lovingkindness. In Jesus' name I pray. Amen.

PRAYER 164 - DWELLING ON THE PAST

Holy Father, I started dwelling on the past again. The pains, the struggles, the hurtful things. They came on me so quickly. But oh, Holy Spirit, thank you for sounding the alarm for me to stop and be still. To hush and be quiet. To listen. Amen.

PRAYER 165 - MIRACLES HIDDEN AWAY
Lord Jesus, bring to my mind remembrances of the good things you have done for me, blessings I had forgotten about, small miracles hidden away, far back in my past. They are all there. So many of them, how could I forget? Let me count them again, and again, and again. In Jesus' name. Amen.

PRAYER 166 - THE DOORS OF MY LIPS
Holy Spirit, thank you for setting a guard over my mouth to keep watch over the door of my lips. "Let the words of my mouth, and the meditation of my heart, be acceptable in thy sight, O Lord, my strength, and my redeemer." Amen.

PRAYER 167 - THE ENTRY GATE
Holy Spirit, unleash within me miracle faith, unexplainable peace and a passion for holy living. Help me to make your word the entry gate into every day of my life. Amen.

PRAYER 168 - PRODIGAL CHILD
Holy Father, set this prodigal child free from their sinful lifestyle. Save them. Give them a new heart. Put your Holy Spirit in them. Take out their old heart of stone and give them a new heart of flesh. Birth in them the spirit of godliness and thanksgiving. Destroy the pride and conceit in them as they humble themselves and cry out to you, "God, have mercy upon me, a sinner." In Jesus' name. Amen.

PRAYER 169 - UNSETTLEDNESS
Holy Father, I feel weak in my faith, make me fearless. I feel uncertain and unsettled, make me strong and unafraid. No matter

how great my fears, quiet me with the courage of a little David against Goliath the giant. Amen.

PRAYER 170 - MY DARKEST DAYS

Precious Holy Spirit, as I walk toward the darkest days of my life, help me to walk by faith and not by sight. In the name of Jesus, I refuse to listen to the intimidation, threats and lies of my enemies. Oh God, Thy word alone is truth. Sharper than any two-edged sword. In the name of Jesus. Amen.

PRAYER 171 - LOOK BEHIND TO SEE AHEAD

Lord Jesus Christ, help me to look behind, so I can see ahead. Remind me that what you did back then, you will do it again and again. You are the same yesterday, today and forever. Hallelujah! I am strong in the Lord, and in the power of his might. Amen.

PRAYER 172 - NOT MY SIN, BUT MY SINNING

Holy Father, sometimes my fear of you is greater than my faith in you. I know you forgive me of my sins, but it's not my sins that are dragging me down, it's my sinning. I always repent, but how many times can I be forgiven for doing the same things over and over again?

Satan condemns me and tells me I'm going to hell. But Jesus, you shed your blood on the cross to cover my sins. Father of compassion, God of all mercy, you said, "I am he who blots out your transgressions, and remembers your sins no more."

As far as the east is from the west, so far has he removed our transgressions from us. Amen.

PRAYER 173 - QUIET MY MIND

Holy Father, quiet my mind so I can think your thoughts. Let your voice drown out the noise of all the distractions around me.

Let me hear you say, "Peace be still." Let me hear you say, "Mountain, be removed and cast into the sea." Let me hear you say, "Don't cry." In Jesus' name. Amen.

PRAYER 174 - WELL DONE GOOD SERVANT

Lord Jesus, Let me hear you say, "Go in peace, your faith has made you whole." Let me hear you say, "Do not let your heart be troubled." Let me hear you say, "I am going away, but I will come again unto you." Let me hear you say, "Well done, good and faithful servant, enter into the joy of your Lord." Amen.

PRAYER 175 - TEARS IN A BOTTLE

Holy Father, what use am I? It seems like I'm always broken. Something is always going wrong. Something is always the matter. I want to help others, but how can I when I can't even seem to help myself? Sometimes I cry every day.

But I almost forgot. You collect all my tears that fall. You store them everyone in a bottle. You make a note of every drop in your book. You keep track of every sorrow. You hear my every heartbeat, you feel my every heartache, you know my every heartbreak. I am thankful. In Jesus' name. Amen.

PRAYER 176 - APPLE OF YOUR EYE

Lord, sometimes I lose my way. I lose track of myself, but you never forget who I am, and what I am and where I am. You know the worst about me, but you always see the best in me. You keep me as the apple of your eye. You hide me under the shadow of your wing. You raise me up on wings as eagles. Praise your name. Amen.

PRAYER 177 - THE CLOUDS THE DUST

Lord God, You make the clouds the dust under your feet and

hold me tight in your arms as you carry me every step of the way. Holy Father, I raise my hands, I bend my knees, I bow my head, I lift up my voice, "Holy, holy, holy Lord, God of power and might. Heaven and earth are full of your glory. Holy, holy, holy. Amen."

PRAYER 178 - FAITH IS A FORCE

Holy Father, I keep forgetting. Remind me that faith is not a feeling, it's a force. It's not what I can see, or feel, or hear ahead of me, it's what I can barely see, and feel and hear inside of me. Not with my mind's mind, but with my heart's mind.

That is why I trust in with all my heart. That is why I hide your word in my heart that I might not sin against you. That is why I love you with all of my soul, all of my strength, all of my mind. That is why I search for you, so that I may be found of you. In Jesus' mighty name. Amen.

PRAYER 179 - FAITH THAT RUSHES

Holy Spirit, empower me, not with a faith that sits back to see what happens, but empower me with your mighty faith that rushes me ahead to make things happen. Fill me with faith that commands, "Mountains of defiance and resistance, mountains uncrossable, move aside, crumble yourselves into the depths of the sea." Amen.

PRAYER 180 - FAITH IN-BETWEEN FAITH

Lord Jesus Christ, give me faith to be born again with. Give me faith to take my last breath with. But most of all, give me faith in-between faith to live with. Give me your righteousness that is by faith from first to last, just as it is written: "The righteous will live by faith." Amen.

PRAYER 181 - MY MIND IS RACING

Holy Father, I'm exhausted. I'm worn out. I can't hold up my head, I can't keep my eyes open, I can't move a single muscle. I'm lying here in bed perfectly still and my mind is racing 90 miles an hour.

My mouth is shut. But my brain won't shut up. The white noise of the fan is lulling me to sleep, but it's not loud enough. Father, it's not that I can't get comfortable, I just can't stay there more than a minute.

The Lord is my shepherd; I shall not want. He maketh me to lie down in green pastures: he leadeth me beside the still waters... Amen.

PRAYER 182 - ATTACK OF MY ENEMY

Holy Father, I lift up my heart and my hands to you. I praise you because of your faithfulness and never-ending love for me. Thank you Father because you defend me against every attack of my enemy. Help me when I have doubts and fears to remember the power of your presence and know that you are only waiting for me to call on you. Amen.

PRAYER 183 - REIGN OVER ME

Lord Jesus, thank you for the abundant life that you give me as I hope and trust in you. Help me to make you the Lord of my life and let you reign over me and everything I do. Thank you for hearing and answering my prayers and that I can call on you anytime and experience your presence and the comfort of the Holy Spirit. In Jesus' name. Amen.

PRAYER 184 - OPEN HEART OPEN MIND

Holy Father, help me to have an open heart and an open mind toward things and people I don't understand. Help me to be cheerful and kind and to know how to relate to people and be encouraging and supportive and know the right things to say and do. In your precious name. Amen.

PRAYER 185 - DISTRACTED BY TRIVIAL

Lord Jesus, cover me with your presence and awesome power. Help me to seek you moment by moment and not get discouraged or distracted by things that are trivial and unimportant.

Holy Father, I want to draw nearer and nearer to you, and further and further away from the things of this world. In Jesus' name I pray. Amen.

PRAYER 186 - EMBRACE MY TRIALS

Holy Father, help me to remember that my trials and tests are there to prove my faith in you and make me stronger. Help me not to resist them or resent them, but embrace them as my highest praise and thanksgiving to you. Amen.

PRAYER 187 - LITTLE MIRACLES

Holy Father, open my eyes so that I can find you everywhere I look. In my failures, in my doubts and fears, in my anxieties and uneasiness and in my past joys and victories that I had forgotten about. I didn't see them then, but now they are so plain and clear in my sight. In Jesus' name. Amen.

PRAYER 188 - THE GLORIOUS RICHES

Holy Father, reveal in me the glorious riches of your Son, the Hope of Glory. Amen.

PRAYER 189 - MY PRAYERS GO SILENT

Holy Father, I need your help with my prayer life. I want to learn how to pray only those prayers you will answer for me. You said that sometimes my prayers go silent because I waste them on wrong things.

But then you said that as long as I keep seeking your righteous kingdom first, you will keep on giving me everything I need, according to your glorious riches in Christ Jesus. Amen.

PRAYER 190 - YOUR PERFECT PRAYER

Holy Father, thank you for teaching me your perfect prayer, The Lord's prayer. I pray it over and over again, no matter where I am, who I'm with, or what I'm doing. Sometimes I pray it loudly. Sometimes I sing it in a song. Mostly, I just whisper it silently in my heart. Amen.

PRAYER 191 - IN MY DEEPEST WOES

Holy Father, I'm not here to ask you for something, I'm here to thank you for everything. You've done so much for me, there's nowhere to start. In every direction I look, you've always been there beside me. In my greatest joys and my deepest woes. In my happiest moments and my loneliest hours. And when I couldn't see you then, I can see you now. In your precious name. Amen.

PRAYER 192 - STAND STILL

Almighty God, thank you for your words, "Ye shall not need to fight in this battle: set yourselves, stand ye still, and see the salvation of the Lord with you...fear not, nor be dismayed...go out against them: for the Lord will be with you. For Thine is the kingdom, and the power, and the glory forever. Amen."

PRAYER 193 - UNANSWERED PRAYER

Holy Father, I am in a hurry again today, and I want you to get into a hurry with me. I've prayed about this situation over and over again. I got past asking why a long time ago. That really doesn't matter anymore, but I can't help asking when? I'm sure I don't need to know the answer to that. I guess I'm just trying to remind you to hurry up.

I thought you would have answered this prayer before now. It seems to me there have been a lot of good opportunities. You know this is not a selfish prayer for me. It's for somebody else I love more than life, and to watch them suffer breaks my heart.

The wait is wearing all of us down. Please don't let it go on much longer. Just let your joy and peace and assurance overflow in my heart and mind and spirit by the power of your Holy Spirit. Amen.

PRAYER 194 - CATCH ME

Holy Father, where can I go and you won't already be there waiting to catch me if I fall apart, find me if I lose my way and restore me, if I fail to measure up? Nowhere. In the name of My Father, His Son and the Holy Ghost. Amen.

PRAYER 195 - NEVER-ENDING Love

Holy Father, only in your presence is joyfulness, peaceful-ness, restfulness and your never-ending lovingkindness. All praise be to the God and Father of our Lord Jesus Christ, Father of compassion and God of all comfort, I want to live in your presence. Amen.

PRAYER 196 - THE TRUTH

Holy Father, I've been listening to fake news, half truths and honest lies so long until I don't know if I can even recognize the truth when I hear it. But thank God! Jesus, you said, "I am the way, the truth and the life."

You said, "You will know the truth and the truth will set you free." You said the Holy Spirit is the Spirit of truth and when he comes, he will guide you into all truth. Lord, you prayed to the Father for us, "Sanctify them through thy truth, thy word is truth." In Jesus' name. Amen.

PRAYER 197 - HIDE YOUR WORD

Holy Spirit of God, help me to read your word every day. Help me to study your word, memorize you word, speak your word and hide your word in my heart so that I will hear the truth, know the truth, believe the truth and say the truth. In Jesus' name I pray. Amen.

PRAYER 198 - OVERCOME MY UNBELIEF

Holy Father, I know nothing is impossible with you. I believe in you with all of my heart, but I'm having trouble trusting in you for myself.

I know you hear me when I pray. I know you can rescue me, I know you can deliver me. I know you can set me free. I just don't know for certain if you will, or at least when you will. Lord, I do believe. Help me to overcome my unbelief! In Jesus' name. Amen.

PRAYER 199 - HEAVENS ARE BRASS

Holy Father, I'm praying, I'm believing and I'm hoping, but the heavens are brass. The showers of blessings have fallen prey to rain clouds full of dust and ashes. The earth beneath my feet has become an iron rock. I can't even sow seed for a harvest. Lord, help me to know what to do. In your name I pray. Amen.

PRAYER 200 - I'M BEGINNING TO SEE

Lord, I know that faith is believing and not seeing. I can do that. But trust is seeing and not receiving and that's where I am fighting for my life.

I can believe in a miracle for someone else, I just can't believe in one for me. But Father, my hands are raised, I'm reaching for you. I'm offering the sacrifice of praise with a spirit of heaviness. And now, at last, after all this while, I'm beginning to see... Amen.

PRAYER 201 - OUTSTRETCHED ARM

O, Lord God, I see it now, You've polished the heavens of brass and made them shine like the brightness of your glory. I look, and all I can see in them now is the reflection of your mighty hand and outstretched arm reaching for me. I feel your breath, I sense your warmth, I know your touch. Praise to thee almighty God! Amen!

PRAYER 202 - MUSTARD-SIZE SEED

Holy Father, the barren iron beneath my feet has become the solid rock on which I stand, unmovable, unshakable, unwavering. And at last, the mustard-size seeds I planted before have returned. Some thirty, some sixty and some a hundredfold. Holy Father, For thine is the kingdom, and the power, and the glory, forever. Amen.

PRAYER 203 - CATCH MY BREATH

Holy Father, help me to stop right here, right now. Help me to catch my breath. Help me to be still long enough for my patience to catch up. I've been going so hard, so fast, for so long until I've lost track of where I am in the moment.

And all this time, while my life has been standing still, I've been running in place trying to get ahead. I'm frustrated and I'm tired, and now I see I've quickly gotten nowhere, trying to go my own way. Lord Jesus Christ, Son of God, have mercy upon me.

In your name I pray. Amen.

PRAYER 204 -PERFECT STORM INSIDE ME

Holy Father, While my mind is racing and my heart is pulsing and my head is pounding, speak to this perfect storm raging within me... "Peace. Be still!" Amen

PRAYER 205 - JESUS COME QUICKLY

Lord Jesus Christ, Son of God, come quickly. Come in golden splendor, in awesome majesty. Exalted in power and glory. Adorned in purity. Amen.

PRAYER 206 - SECURE ON HOLY GROUND

Holy Father, as I walk by faith and not by sight, help me to take comfort that the solid rock on which I stand rests secure on holy ground. All praise be to the God and Father of our Lord Jesus Christ, the Father of compassion, the God of all comfort. Amen.

PRAYER 207 - EMOTIONS ON EDGE

Holy Father, help me to stop and be still, if just for a moment. My emotions are on edge. I'm beginning to feel my attitude drifting off course. I've gotten so caught up in the crowd mentality until I've nearly lost sight of the mind of Christ. But you set me free! Amen!

PRAYER 208 - CONFRONTATION

Jesus, help me to remember that instead of becoming con-frontational in personal strife, you always stayed compassionate. Instead of becoming combative in civil strife, you always remained compliant. In Jesus' name I pray. Amen.

PRAYER 209 - HELP ME TO BE YOU

Lord Jesus Christ, Son of God, have mercy upon me. Help me to be you to those around me who have lost their way. Help me to be your sense of direction and not their cause of distraction. Help me to lose myself, so I can win them to you. In Jesus' name. Amen.

PRAYER 210 - MIGHTY RUSHING WIND

Holy Father, instead of listening to so many conflicting voices, help me to listen to your still small voice. Instead of hearing all those confusing sounds, help me to hear the sound of your mighty rushing wind filling the place where I am. Amen.

PRAYER 211 - LIVE THE GOLDEN RULE

Holy Father, today, help me to live the Golden Rule to your highest expectation. For yours, O Lord, is the greatness, The power and the glory. The victory and the majesty. For all that is in heaven and in earth is Yours. Amen.

PRAYER 212 - HUMBLE STRENGTH

Holy Father, give me humble strength. Help me to realize that the weaker I am in myself, the stronger I am in you. In Jesus' name. Amen.

PRAYER 213 - PAST JOYS AND VICTORIES

Holy Father, open my eyes so that I can find you everywhere I look. In my failures, in my doubts and fears, in my anxieties and uneasiness, but most of all in my past joys and victories that I had forgotten about. In Jesus' name I pray. Amen.

PRAYER 214 - YOU HEAL ME

Holy Father, I praise you and I adore you. I bless and exalt your holy name. I worship you because you heal me. You forgive me. You comfort me and guide every step I take along the way. You protect me and provide for me. You prosper and empower me with your Holy Spirit. In Jesus' name. Amen.

PRAYER 215 - ALWAYS BE READY

You said that "...the Son of Man will come at an hour when you do not expect him." So, Lord, help me to always be ready, watching and winning to you those who are reaching out to be made whole. For Thine is the kingdom and the power and the glory, forever. Amen.

PRAYER 216 - DEFEND MYSELF

Holy Father, thank you for the armor of God you have given me to defend myself against every evil of Satan. Cover me Lord with your presence. Cover me Lord with your Righteousness, Peace, Faith, Salvation, The Word of God and Prayer. Even so Lord Jesus, come quickly! Amen

PRAYER 217 - MEDICAL TROOPS

Holy Father, all of us put together cannot express enough gratitude to our countless medical troops - doctors, nurses, technicians, researchers and support - who have deployed themselves against this dreaded pandemic. But we can all pray.

Lord God, make them our last prayer before we fall asleep tonight. Make them our first prayer when we wake up in the morning. And in those empty, thoughtless moments that pop up throughout the day, may we cry out to you for them.

Almighty God, anoint these, your angels of mercy with a supernatural armor of immunity and resistance against this murderous enemy they battle. Spare them their lives so that they may spare other's theirs. Lord Jesus Christ, Son of God, have mercy upon us. Amen.

PRAYER 218 - MY CHILDREN'S RESPECT

Holy Father, as long as my children live, may they only know and show respect, humility, integrity, forgiveness and gratitude. In Jesus' name. Amen.

PRAYER 219 - MY RACING HEARTBEATS

Lord Jesus Christ, quiet my unsettled spirit today. Ease my racing heartbeats. Help me to realize that this is holy ground I'm standing on, and that these, my uncertain circumstances, are the sanctuary where you want me to worship you in Spirit and in truth. Amen.

PRAYER 220 - FAMILY, SHINING LIGHTS

Holy Father, I pray for my family today. I call out each of their names to you right now. Free them from all worries and fear. Crush the uncertainties and doubts that come against them. Fill them instead with the power, and greatness, and presence of your mighty Holy Spirit.

God, make us all shining lights of your glory, caring and kind and compassionate to those around us. Let us overflow with thanksgiving and praise to you so that the words we speak, the thoughts we think, and the things we do will always be to the honor, glory and majesty of your holy name. Father, fill us with all joy and peace as we trust in you. Amen.

PRAYER 221 - CONFIDENT AND COURAGEOUS

Holy Father, pour out all of your goodness and favor and blessings upon my family today. Guard and protect each one of us from all harm and danger. Keep us healthy and well against all sickness and disease. Lord God, prosper us with your spiritual wealth. Grant us all of the good things that no amount of money on earth can buy - love, joy, friendship, forgiveness...

Father, make us rich in kindness, mercy and forgiveness toward others. Let the truth and power of your holy word live in us and cause us to walk in your wisdom and understanding. Lead us in steps of righteousness.

Lord God, overflow us with your joy and peace and hope and faith and trust. Keep us confident and courageous in your mighty power. Lord of Lords, Prince of Peace, everlasting Father, clothe us with your salvation and adorn us with your robe of righteousness. In Jesus' name. Amen.

PRAYER 222 - EVERY DREAM

Holy Spirit, Give me the self-confidence and inner persuasion that I will accomplish every dream and goal you have laid out for my life. In Jesus' name I pray. Amen.

PRAYER 223 - WHISPERS OF WISDOM

Holy Spirit, you are the breath of God. Help me to slow down and breathe and relax and focus all of my thoughts on you. Help me to stay quiet and listen for your whispers of discerning and wisdom. Give me spirit eyes to see what you see and trust totally in what you say and tell me to do. Amen.

PRAYER 224 - YOU ARE CLOSE BESIDE ME

Holy Father, you are God Most High, exalted above everything. You bring life back to the dead and create never before things out of nothing. Help me to know that in this moment, you are close beside me. No matter what, your arms will always reach out to me. In Jesus' name I pray. Amen.

PRAYER 225 FAMILY PRAYER

Holy Father, I pray for my family today. I call out each of their names to you right now. Free them from all worries and fear. Crush the uncertainties and doubts that come against them. Fill them instead with the power and greatness and presence of your mighty Holy Spirit. In Jesus' name. Amen.

PRAYER 226 - SHINING GLORY

Holy Father, make me a shining light of your glory, caring and kind and compassionate to those around me. Let me overflow with thanksgiving and praise to you, so that the words I speak, the thoughts I think and the things I do always be to the honor and glory and majesty of your holy name. Father, fill me with all joy and peace as I trust in you. Amen.

PRAYER 227 - SELF-CONFIDENCE

Holy Spirit, Give me the self-confidence and inner persuasion that I will accomplish every dream and goal you have laid out for my life. In Jesus' name I pray. Amen.

PRAYER 228 - THIS PERFECT STORM

Holy Father, help me to stop right here, right now. Help me to catch my breath. Help me to be still long enough for my patience to catch up.

I've been going so hard, so fast, for so long until I've lost track of where I am in the moment. And all this time, while my life has been standing still, I've been running in place trying to get ahead. I'm frustrated and I'm tired and now I see I've quickly gotten nowhere, trying to go my own way.

Lord Jesus Christ, while my mind is racing and my heart is pulsing and my head is pounding, speak to this perfect storm raging within me, "Peace. Be still." Amen.

PRAYER 229 - STAY QUIET AND LISTEN

Holy Spirit, you are the breath of God. Help me to slow down and breathe, and relax, and focus all of my thinking and attention on you. Help me to stay quiet and listen for your whispers of discerning and wisdom. Give me spirit eyes to see what you see and trust totally in what you say and tell me to do. Amen.

PRAYER 230 - THE BATTLE IS NOT YOURS

Lord Jesus, I await your coming with great victory and triumphant glory! The battles before me are overwhelming, but Holy Father, you promised, "The battle is not yours, but the Lord's." Help me Holy Father to be ready and stand my ground with immovable and unshakable trust and faith. Even so, Lord Jesus come. Amen.

PRAYER 231 - YOUR AWESOME DEEDS

Holy Father, I trust you, I hope in you, I believe in you, I put my faith in you. I lean on you, I listen to you, I obey you. I love you. I tell of your greatness and mercy and awesome deeds. Let me speak in praise of you all day long. Amen.

PRAYER 232 - MIGHTY RUSHING WIND

Holy Father, instead of listening to so many conflicting voices, help me to listen to your still small voice. Instead of hearing all those confusing sounds, help me to hear the sound of your mighty rushing wind filling the place where I stand. In Jesus' name I pray. Amen.

PRAYER 233 - DECISIONS

Holy Father, I need your wisdom. I have some choices to make and I want to do the right thing. These are not easy decisions

I'm facing, they will have repercussions that I'm deeply concerned about.

I have great responsibilities that are causing me to think I have to hang on, but I really feel in my heart of hearts that I need to let go.

God, I know that you balance every choice with consequences, but even good choices by one person can sometimes create bad consequences for someone else. Lord, I'm praying.

Help me to take the leap of faith for myself, and trust you to take care of everyone and everything else behind me. You said that, "The steps of a good man are ordered by the Lord and He delights in his way." In Jesus' name I pray. Amen.

PRAYER 234 - COMING WITH THE CLOUDS

Lord Jesus Christ, Son of God, make me your crown of rejoicing at your coming in great splendor and glory. Behold, You are coming with the clouds, and every eye will see you. Come quickly, O Lord. I yearn to see you in all your golden splendor, and awesome majesty, exalted in power and glory, adorned in purity. Amen and Amen!!

PRAYER 235 - SALVATION FOR LOVED ONE

Holy Father, I am asking you for a miracle of deliverance and salvation in our family. All the rest of us love you and serve you and trust you. But this one has a hard heart, a spirit of defiance and resistance. Lord Jesus, only you can quell the darkness in them and turn their life around 180°.

After so long, it almost seems to be an impossibility, but I know there is nothing too hard for the Lord. With you all things are possible. Holy Father, you have a storehouse of more miracles than can be counted. Lord Jesus, give our family one of those miracles today. We thank you in Jesus' name. Amen.

PRAYER 236 - YIELD TO YOUR WILL

Holy Father, help me to accept today just as it comes. Help me to not waste my time wishing for a different set of circumstances, but help me to trust you enough to yield to your will and purpose for my life. In Jesus' name. Amen.

PRAYER 237 - TO TOUCH ONE PERSON

Holy Father, help me to touch at least one person today with your caring, compassion and kindness. Let the words I speak and the things I do, plant in them the seeds of hope, joy and peace that will change their lives forever. In Jesus' name I pray. Amen.

PRAYER 238 - DIVINE FAVOR

Holy Father, surround me with your blessings and divine favor today. Pour out every good thing that is yours upon my life. Let me walk in the abundance of your grace and mercy and lovingkindness. Let the goodwill and favor of everyone I encounter today come upon me. Amen.

PRAYER 239 - WHERE CAN I GO?

Holy Father, Where can I go and you won't already be there waiting to catch me if I fall apart, find me if I lose my way and restore me, if I fail to measure up? Nowhere. In the name of My Father, His Son and the Holy Ghost. Amen.

PRAYER 240 - SPEAK THE TRUTH

Holy Spirit of God, help me to read your word every day. Help me to study your word, memorize you word, speak your word and hide your word in my heart so that I will hear the truth, know the truth, believe the truth and speak the truth. In Jesus' name I pray. Amen.

PRAYER 241 - FAMILY PRAYER

Holy Father, I entrust every member of my family into your loving hands. I release them into your provision and protective care. I pray that they will always pray the sinner's prayer and walk in your faith and peace, hope and joy, thankfulness and lovingkindness. In Jesus' name. Amen.

PRAYER 242 - LYING LIPS

Holy Father, deliver my soul from those with lying lips and a deceitful tongue. Lord, help me to impress upon my children that freedom of speech never allows anyone the freedom to lie. Holy Father, make me righteous through the truth of thy Word. In Jesus' name. Amen.

PRAYER 243 - RAISED IMMORTAL

Holy Father, always be the centerpoint of my innermost being. Be the life and breath of me, so that when the last trumpet sounds, I will be raised imperishable, immortal and eternal. Be ready, because the Son of man will come when you do not expect him. Amen!

PRAYER 244 - SALVATION FOR LOVED ONE

Holy Father, open my loved one's heart to forgiveness. Let them experience your blessings and lovingkindness. Help them to come to know you in the way of salvation and receive your goodness into their life.

Holy Spirit, become their constant friend and companion. Lord, speak to them. Give them a heart of flesh and take away their stony heart. Cause them to bow before you in humble submission and obedience. Protect them and keep them safe from all harm.

Lord, watch over them throughout every day. Come into

their thoughts. And in their quiet moments, reveal yourself to them. I pray that the measure of faith within them will spring to life and awaken them to peace and joyfulness and salvation, in Jesus' name I pray. Amen.

PRAYER 245 - LIVE BY THE TRUTH

Holy Father, help me to always live my life by the truth of your Holy Word. You said that you hate "a lying tongue and a false witness who speaks lies." God, forbid that I would ever ally or align myself with anything you hate.

Lord, in your Word there are no alternative facts. In your Word, the truth is non-negotiable. In your Word, you cannot lie with impunity. Holy Father, remind me everyday that anything less than the whole truth and nothing but the truth, so help me God, is a lie.

Jesus, you said, "I am the way, the truth, and the life; no man comes unto the Father, but by me." Lord Jesus Christ, Son of God, just as I am, I come to thee. Amen.

PRAYER 246 - TEETERING EMOTIONS

Holy Father, I am trusting you. Yet, so many unanswered questions are starting to elbow their way in. Doubts and uncertainties are slowly beginning to stir up stress and strain inside me.

Teetering emotions of insecurity and uneasiness are starting to sway me away from your perfect ease and certainty. Lord Jesus, I cry out to you to command back to me, "Peace be still! Arise and be healed! Your faith has made you whole!" Amen!

PRAYER 247 - PERFECT PEACE

Holy Father, you promised as long as I keep my mind stayed on you, you will keep your perfect peace encircled around me. Peace of God that transcends all understanding, guard my heart and shield my mind against every assault and every insult of my enemies. In Jesus' name I pray. Amen.

PRAYER 248 - YOU CANNOT LIE

Holy Father, I'm troubled because now, for too many, true or false has become a multiple choice question. Lord, help us to remember that in your Word there are no alternative facts. In your Word, the truth is non-negotiable. In your Word, you cannot lie with impunity.

Holy Father, remind us everyday that anything less than the whole truth and nothing but the truth, so help me God, is no truth at all. In Jesus' name I pray. Amen.

PRAYER 249 - HAVE AN OPEN MIND

Holy Father, help me to have an open heart and mind toward others I don't agree with or understand. Especially those I don't like. Help me to have the mind of Christ and know how to relate to them with your compassion and love regardless of how they treat me. Lord, help me to know when to keep silent and when to not say anything. Help me to know how to listen and stay quiet. And help me to do it. Amen.

PRAYER 250 - CHOICES AND CONSEQUENCES

Holy Father, help me to stand firm in my values and convictions, but respect other's rights to choose their own and live as they please. Lord, help me to remember that you balance all of our choices with consequences and only you are the righteous judge, not me. Lord, you have called me to a higher standard, help me to keep reaching with faithfulness and perseverance. In Jesus' name. Amen.

PRAYER 251 - THE PRECIOUS BLOOD

Holy Father, help us to realize that the blood of protesters and police officers can only bring us and them a false sense of self-righteousness. God forbid, lest we all trample over the precious Blood of the Lamb. Lord Jesus Christ, have mercy. Amen.

PRAYER 252 - ALL AROUND ME

Holy Father, when I open my eyes and look, I see you all around me. When I close my eyes and think of you, I feel your presence in me. In Jesus' name. Amen.

PRAYER 253 - WHAT ABOUT THIS?

Holy Father, uncertainties and indecisions are swirling all around me. I'm overwhelmed with the thoughts of what about this? And what about that? And what if this? And what if that? Lord Jesus, drown all of my doubts and fears in a single drop of your crying tears. Amen.

PRAYER 254 - ASLEEP IN MY YESTERDAYS

Holy Father, I thank you for those who are now asleep in my yesterdays, but they are very much alive in my todays. They gave me fun and laughter, joy and delight. They instilled in me respect and gratitude, integrity and my love for life. They taught me strength through weakness and success from failure.

Lord God, they taught me faith and hope and love. Some of them adopted me and I adopted them. Many of them have been long gone, but none of them are long forgotten. Part of them is still a part of who I am today, and will be tomorrow. Lord Jesus, thank you for my parents, my teachers, my pastors, my coaches, my leaders. Help me to carry on their legacy of truth and faith-fulness and pass it on to those who go ahead of me. Amen.

Prayer 255 - REPENT OF MY SINS

Holy Father, search my heart. I repent of my sins and turn to you. I strive with all of my being to follow and obey you, believe and trust in you, hope and have faith in you.

Lord God, you are my strength and defense against every enemy that seeks to attack and destroy my faith and hope in you. Amen.

PRAYER 256 - FOR MY HEALING

Lord God, You said, "I am the Lord that heals you. I will take away sickness from among you. I am your God, I will strengthen and help you. I will uphold you with my righteous right hand, and by my stripes you were healed." In the name of the Father, the Son and the Holy Spirit, heal me I pray. Amen.

PRAYER 257 - EVERY LIGHT THAT SHINES

Holy Father, every step I take, you encounter me with your majesty and great glory. Every angel and heavenly creature sings of your awesome splendor. Every light that shines in the night shines on you. Amen.

PRAYER 258 - MY ALL AND ALL

Holy Father, I put my all and all in you. Oh, the depth of the riches of the knowledge of God! How unsearchable his judgments, his ways beyond finding out. Amen!!

PRAYER 259 - WEIGHT OF MY TROUBLES

Holy Father, help me to not miss the joy of your presence because I am too busy trying to take on the weight of my troubles. Lord, forgive me for trying to take back what I have already given to you. Open my eyes so that I will only see your goodness. Unstop my ears so that I will only hear your praises. In Jesus' name. Amen.

PRAYER 260 - ACCEPTING, FORGIVING ME

Holy Father, thank you for accepting me and forgiving me. Thank you for healing me and comforting me. Thank you for blessing me, indwelling me and empowering me. Most of all, thank you for loving me. "For God so loved the world that he gave his only begotten son." Amen!

PRAYER 261 - THE JESUS PRAYER

"Lord Jesus Christ, Son of God, have mercy upon me, a sinner." Amen.

PRAYER 262 - I WILL OVERFLOW

God of hope, fill me with all joy and peace as I trust in you, so that I will overflow with faith, hope and love by the power of the Holy Spirit. Amen.

PRAYER 263 - DISTRESS OF NATIONS

Holy Father, have mercy on me. While the world tempest is raging, distress of nations is looming, you said you will hide me under the shadow of the Almighty. You will stretch over me with your wings, you will be my refuge, my rock and fortress. Amen.

PRAYER 264 - NO HARM COME NEAR ME

Holy Father, you said you would deliver me from the pestilence in darkness and the plague that lays waste in the day. You said that no harm would come near me, even when a thousand may fall by my side and ten thousand at my right hand. Amen.

PRAYER 265 - SIDETRACKED

Holy Spirit, You are my counselor and teacher and guide. Release my mind and thoughts from negative forces of ungodly distractions.

Holy Father, help me to turn my full attention towards you so that my problems will fade into insignificance and lose all their strength to sidetrack me away from your indwelling empowerment. In Jesus' name. Amen.

PRAYER 266 - NEW IDEAS

Holy Father, raise me up to shine like the stars. Let your brightness radiate from my innermost being. Let my words be uplifting and encouraging, my ideas new and exciting. Let my actions be powerful demonstration of your kindness and compassion and care to all.

Lord, let others see you in me and want for themselves the glorious riches of Christ Jesus. Let it happen today. Amen.

PRAYER 267 - ALWAYS BRING ME THROUGH

Holy Father lead me with joy and gladness so that I will praise your name forever and ever. Help me to trust you to bring me though the hard places and remember that you never let bad things happen to me, but you will always bring me thorough them as I hope and trust in you. In Jesus' name I pray. Amen.

PRAYER 268 - NEGATIVITY

Lord Jesus, help me to overcome complaining and speaking negative words. Help me to substitute negativity with cheerfulness and complaining with thankfulness. Help me to discover firsthand that the joy of the Lord really is my strength! Amen.

PRAYER 269 - FOOTSTEPS OF FAITH

Holy Father, help me to follow in the footsteps of the faith of your son Abraham. Help me to trust you like he did without question or hesitation. Help me to always remember that you are our Jehovah Jirah, the Lord our God who provides! Amen.

PRAYER 270 - DOORS OF DOUBT

Holy Spirit of God, help me to break through the doors of doubt by the prayers I pray and your words I hide in my heart that I might not sin against you. Help me to filter out all the bad in my life by clinging to the precious blood Jesus shed on the cross. In your precious name I pray. Amen.

PRAYER 271 - MY POUNDING HEARTBEAT

Holy Father, I kneel in my heart and feel the warmth of your arms reaching around me. Son of God, you are the great shepherd. Pick me up and carry me like the lost little lamb that I am.

Let the pounding of my heartbeat quiet down to the soft, silent rhythm of yours. In Jesus' name I pray. Amen.

PRAYER 272 - MY TREMBLING HANDS

Holy Father, let your gentleness absorb my unsettledness, your soothing touch my tenseness. Lord Jesus, drown out all of my doubts and fears with a single drop of the dying tears you shed for me in your darkest hours on the Cross. I raise up my trembling hands to feel the touch of your nail-scarred hands. Amen.

PRAYER 273 - STRESSED OUT

Holy Father, I have a tendency to want to go back to yesterday, or fret about tomorrow. Help me to just come back home to today. Help me to see you in the here and now and not try to look for you in the nowhere places of my ideas and imaginations that are stressing me out, and will never come to pass. In Jesus' name. Amen.

PRAYER 274 - MY MIND

Holy Father, help me to see things more and more through your perspective and not through my mindset, the way I want to see them and the way I want them to happen. Let the light of your presence so fully fill my mind that I will view all the things happening around me through the power of your Holy Spirit and not through my weaknesses, shortcomings and failures. Amen.

PRAYER 275 - FOOTPRINTS

Holy Father, be my guide and sure direction today, so that all of my footsteps will fit perfectly inside all of your footprints. In Jesus' name. Amen.

PRAYER 276 - CHANGES

Holy Father, I don't like changes. I've been able to avoid a lot of them for a long time, but now there's no escaping. I've been comfortable where I've been, but now I'm not sure where that was. I've been looking back, but there's no normal to go back to.

I've been looking ahead for the new normal, but I don't think there's going to be one. Holy Father, help me to just close my eyes and look at you. In Jesus' name. Amen.

PRAYER 277 - I REPENT

Holy Father, I confess my sins to you. Help me to repent and forever forsake them. Help me to walk in the beauty of your holiness. In Jesus' name I pray. Amen.

PRAYER 278 - PRAYER FOR MILITARY

Holy Father, I pray for our military troops tonight. Guard them, as they guard us. Watch over them, as they watch over us. Protect them, as they protect us. Keep them safe, as they keep us safe. In Jesus' name. Amen.

PRAYER 279 - GOD'S ACCEPTANCE

Holy Father, thank you for accepting me and forgiving me. Thank you for healing me and comforting me. Thank you for blessing me, indwelling me and empowering me. Most of all, thank you for loving me. "For God so loved the world that he gave his only begotten son." Amen!

PRAYER 280 - TROUBLES

Holy Father, help me to not miss the joy of your presence because I am too busy trying to take on the weight of my troubles. Lord, forgive me for trying to take back what I have already given to you.

Holy Spirit, open my eyes so that I will only see the righteous path you are leading me through. Unstop my ears so that I will only hear your truth and wisdom speaking clearly to my mind and heart. In Jesus' name. Amen.

PRAYER 281 - THE DEPTH OF RICHES

Holy Father, every step I take, you encounter me with your majesty and great glory. Every angel and heavenly creature sings of your awesome splendor. Every light that shines in the night shines on you.

Holy Father, I put my all and all in you. Oh, the depth of the riches of the knowledge of God! How unsearchable his judgments, his ways beyond finding out. Amen!!

PRAYER 282 - EVERY ENEMY

Holy Father, search my heart. I repent of my sins and turn to you. I strive with all of my being to follow and obey you, believe and trust in you, hope and have faith in you, for you are my strength and defense against every enemy that seeks to attack and destroy my faith and hope in you. Amen.

PRAYER 283 - INDECISIONS

Holy Father, uncertainties and indecisions are swirling all around me. I'm overwhelmed with the thoughts of what about this? And what about that? And what if this? And what if that? Lord Jesus, drown all of my doubts and fears in a single drop of your dying tears. In Jesus' name. Amen.

PRAYER 284 - HEALED

Lord God, You said, "I am the Lord that heals you. I will take away sickness from among you. I am your God, I will strengthen and help you. I will uphold you with my righteous right hand, and by my stripes you were healed." In the name of the Father, the Son and the Holy Spirit I pray. Amen.

PRAYER 285 - THINGS DON'T GO MY WAY

Father, when things don't go as I hoped and prayed for, speak to me, "My way is easy and my burden is light. I am the Lord your God, I will take hold of your weak hands, I will guide you through every hard and heavy place.

I will go with you to fight for you against all of your enemies and I will give you irreversible victory and triumph. Only hope and trust in me." Amen.

PRAYER 286 - EVERY KNEE WILL BOW

Lord Jesus, I pray your name. I praise your name. I proclaim your name. That at the mention of your name, every knee shall bow, every tongue confess, that Jesus Christ is Lord to the glory of God the Father. Amen.

PRAYER 287 - EVERY BLESSING

Holy Father, I bow my head to reverence your holiness. I raise my hands to receive your righteousness. I close my eyes and ears to block out all of the sights and sounds of worldliness. I open my heart and mind to be filled with every blessing, promise, good and perfect gift that comes from you. In Jesus' name I pray. Amen.

PRAYER 288 - YOUR PATH

Holy Father, help me to pour out more and more of my energy into trusting you today. Help me to focus my attention on the path ahead, that you have laid out for me to follow. In Jesus' name. Amen.

PRAYER 289 - DYING TEARS

Holy Father, let your gentleness absorb my unsettledness, your soothing touch my tenseness. Lord Jesus, drown out all of my doubts and fears with a single drop of the dying tears you shed for me in your darkest hours on the Cross. I raise up my trembling hands to feel the touch of your reaching down, nail-scarred hands. Amen.

PRAYER 290 - HEAVY BURDENS

Lord Jesus, you know the heavy burden I am carrying today. Help me to bury it at the foot of your Cross. Amen.

PRAYER 291 - UNCERTAINTIES

Holy Father, let your purpose prevail in my life. I'm trusting you, but I still deal with uncertainties and self-doubt and insecurities. I need you to assure me that everything will be all right because I trust in you. In Jesus' name. Amen.

PRAYER 292 - GUIDE ME

Holy Spirit, you said you would walk along beside me. Help me today to experience more and more of your calmness and peace. Empower me to resist doubt and unsettledness.

Fill me with your wisdom. Teach me the way that I should take. Guide me along the best pathway for my life. Counsel me, watch over me, encourage me and inspire me. Amen.

PRAYER 293 - UNEASY AND APPREHENSIVE

Lord Jesus, help me to be excited about what lies ahead and not feel uneasy and apprehensive. Calm every doubt and cross out every fear. Fill me with certainty that you are making the way before me. It is not my doing, but your's. Make it wonderful before my eyes. In Jesus' name. Amen.

PRAYER 294 - EXPECTATION

Holy Father help me to develop an environment of expectation and obedience and to believe in my own worthiness to receive a miracle from your miracle working hand. Amen.

PRAYER 295 - I BELIEVE IN MIRACLES

Holy Father, I believe in divine healing. I believe in miracles. I believe you hear and answer prayer. Lord, help me to believe you will hear and answer my prayer, that you will heal me, that you will release a miracle into my life. Lord, I believe, help thou my unbelief. In Jesus' name I pray. Amen.

PRAYER 296 - LORD, WE LEAN ON YOU

Holy Father, we believe in you. We lean on you. We hope in you. We put all of our faith in you. Fill us with all joy and peace as we trust in you, so that we will overflow with faith, hope and love by the power of your Holy Spirit within us. In Jesus' name. Amen.

Prayer 297 - Opening And Closing Doors

Holy Father, thank you for guiding every footstep we take. Thank you for opening doors and closing doors. Help us to know which one is which. In Jesus' name. Amen.

Prayer 298 - Letting Go

Holy Father, instead of trying to control and grasp hold of, help us to receive from you and let go of. Fill us with your blessings, overflow us with your favor and engulf us in your never-ending lovingkindness. In Jesus' name. Amen.

Prayer 299 - Anxiety

Holy Father I praise you that when my anxiety is greater than I can seem to bear, you will comfort me with your joy and gladness. You reach into my being and raise me up. Holy Father, I bow down before you, I kneel in your presence and sing praises to your name O most high. Amen.

Prayer 300 - We Will Escape

Holy Father, deliver us from the darkness of the spiritual forces alive and against us today. Fill us with all of the fullness of the mind of Christ so that we will escape the gravity of this world's evil and ungodliness.

Make us strong in you and in the awesome power of your might. There is none like you, you are our rock and hiding place, our deliverer and redeemer. In Jesus' mighty name we pray! Amen!

Prayer 301 - Problem-Solving Mode

Holy Father, help me not to jump into a problem-solving mode today and try to fix what is only going to frustrate me and weaken my faith in you. Lord, help me to pray and give this situation to you and trust that you will work it out in your own time. In Jesus' name. Amen.

PRAYER 302 - WALK ON HOLY GROUND

Holy Father, in these difficult and uncertain times we stand on your solid ground. We walk on your holy ground. And we thrive and produce your Fruits of the Spirit on the good ground of our hearts. In Jesus' name we pray. Amen.

PRAYER 303 - RESTLESSNESS

Holy Father, Help us to look away from ourselves today and see others who are in trouble and struggling. We pray for a friend who is lost and afraid - give them courage and direction. Overshadow them with your peace and quietness. Becalm their restlessness and uneasiness. Fill them with your peacefulness. In Jesus' name. Amen.

PRAYER 304 - EMPTY HANDS

Holy Father, as I reach out to you with my open, empty hands, I pray to receive the mercy and forgiveness of your sacred, nail scarred hands. Jesus, keep me near the cross. Be my glory ever. Amen.

PRAYER 305 - LOST AND AFRAID

Holy Father, help us to look away from ourselves today and see others who are in trouble and struggling. We pray for a friend who is lost and afraid - give them courage and direction. Overshadow them with your peace and quietness. Becalm their restlessness and uneasiness. Fill them with your peacefulness. Amen.

PRAYER 306 - YOUR MARVELOUS LIGHT

Lord Jesus, bring out those who are in darkness into your marvelous light. Let the brightness of your presence help them to see you clearly, and feel your warmth, and hear your words, "Come to me and I will give you rest." In Jesus' name I pray. Amen.

PRAYER 307 - LEAVE MY PAST BEHIND

Holy Father, help me not to mix my yesterday with today. Help me to leave my past behind and walk away. In Jesus' name I pray. Amen.

PRAYER 308 - FAMILY PRAYER

Holy Father, pour out all of your goodness and favor and blessings upon our family today. Guard and protect them from all harm and danger. Prosper them in their body, mind, soul and spirit. Take away any pain and hurting they are struggling with today, yesterday and tomorrow. Let them only hear and see and feel your touch of peace and calm in their dark moments.

Lord, make them rich in their innermost being with godliness and righteousness. Let the truth and power of your holy Word indwell them and cause them to walk in wisdom and understanding. Lord God, overflow them with your joy and hope and faith and trust.

Keep them confident and courageous in you, free of worry and fear and doubts, and anxiety, full of the peace, power and presence of God the Father, God the Son, and God the Holy Spirit.

Lord God, make them shining lights of your glory. Caring and kind and compassionate to those around them. Let them overflow with thanksgiving and praise to you. Keep their minds always stayed on you. Help them to pray without ceasing and rejoice evermore.

Lord, let the words they speak, the thoughts they think, and the things they do always bring you glory and honor and majesty. Lord Jesus, as they pray and believe in you, bring them through every obstacle and barrier that rises up against them.

Give them miracles and wonders in their lives, miracles of healing and deliverance and especially miracles of perseverance to stand strong and firm, immovable and unshakable against the powers of darkness that come against them. Holy Spirit, pray for them with groanings we cannot utter.

Lord Jesus, Son of God, each of them in their bodies and entire being. Raise them up on Eagles wings above all their pain and struggles. Speak to them, "Peace be still! Rise and be healed, your faith has made you whole!" God of hope fill them with all joy and peace as they trust in you. May they overflow with faith, hope and love by the mighty power of your Holy Spirit.

Holy Father, let my family rest in you and see you fight their enemies and always bring them through to victory. Impart to them the mind of Christ to be a humble and obedient servant. Anoint them to pray the prayers of faith and agreement that will bring them through every battle that wages against them.

Father, keep my family always ready for the day of your coming. Let them see you descend in the clouds of glory. Lord Jesus, come in golden splendor, and awesome majesty, exalted in power and glory, adorned in purity. All praise, honor and glory be to the God and Father of our Lord Jesus Christ. Amen!

PRAYER 309 - PTSD PRAYER

Holy Father, we all agree together for those women and men who struggle and battle against PTSD everyday of their lives. Soldiers, first responders, emergency and trauma personnel and many nameless others.

Lord Jesus, diminish the pain and hurting they are experiencing today, yesterday and tomorrow. Especially when they are attacked, blind out the sights and sounds and smells that are always hurting and wounding them again and again. Let them only hear and see and feel your touch of peace and calm in those dark moments.

Holy Father, fill us all with love and compassion and sensitivity to these brave men and women, our country's greatest patriots and defenders. Bring them to our minds always to guard and defend them with all of our deepest thoughts and prayers. In Jesus' mighty name we pray. Amen.

PRAYER 310 - A PRAYER FOR HEALING

Holy Father, we agree together in prayer for those who are struggling with a medical event today. Breathe your breath of peace and ease and calm into their entire being, heart, mind, soul and spirit. Quiet their emotions and feelings of fear and anxiety.

Lord God, pour out the anointing oil of your healing upon them. Let it cover them from head to toe and saturate every cell of their organs and systems of their body. Release your miracles into their lives. Jesus raise them up from their bed of affliction. Deliver them from every sickness, disease and virus attacking them.

Holy Spirit, comfort their family around them, nourish them with extraordinary hope and faith in you. Speak to all of us, peace be still. In Jesus' name we pray. Amen.

www.ingramcontent.com/pod-product-compliance
Lightning Source LLC
Chambersburg PA
CBHW071838020426
42331CB00007B/1783